KRISHNA MOHAN AVANCHA

AHAAM BRAHMASMI!!!

First edition

This book was professionally typeset on Reedsy.
Find out more at reedsy.com

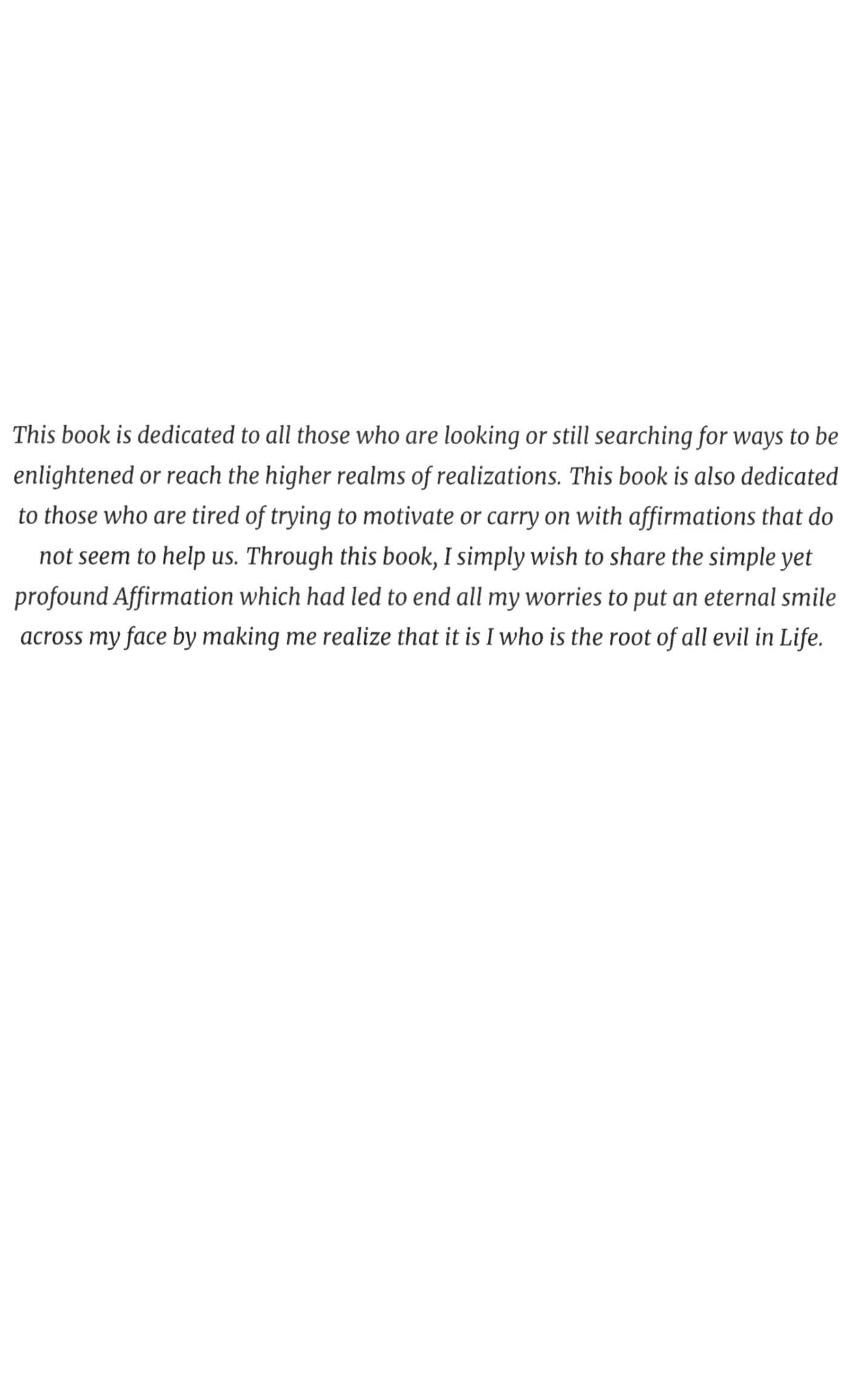

This book is dedicated to all those who are looking or still searching for ways to be enlightened or reach the higher realms of realizations. This book is also dedicated to those who are tired of trying to motivate or carry on with affirmations that do not seem to help us. Through this book, I simply wish to share the simple yet profound Affirmation which had led to end all my worries to put an eternal smile across my face by making me realize that it is I who is the root of all evil in Life.

Contents

1

Introduction

I was led not long ago by the great guru Shree guru, Shree nrisimha Saraswathi through one of his disciples Pujya acharya Ekkirala Bharadwaja writings in the book,' Shri Guru Charitra' about the accounts of the Shree Guru's monumental feats that made me realize this simple and yet profound truth. So these words may be mine but I am just reciting what they have told or taught me as I am merely a speck of dust in his eternal world without whose guidance and help I am forever lost.

Aaham Brahmasmi!!! is the primary Mahavakyas-the short assertions known as the "Incomparable Utterances" from the Upanishads. The others namely being:

1. Prajñānam Brahma (प्रज्ञानम् ब्रह्म) – "Understanding is Brahman," or "Brahman is insight"[web 1] (Aitareya Upanishad 3.3 of the Rig Veda)
2. Ayam Ātmā Brahma (अयम् आत्मा ब्रह्म) – "This Self (Atman) is Brahman" (Mandukya Upanishad 1.2 of the Atharva Veda)
3. Tat Tvam Asi (तत् त्वम् असि) – "That quintessence (tat, alluding to sat, "the Existent" are you" (Chandogya Upanishad 6.8.7 of the Sama Veda)
4. Aham Brahmāsmi (अहम् ब्रह्मास्मि) – "I'm Brahman" (Brihadaranyaka Upanishad 1.4.10 of the Yajur Veda)

They all express the understanding that the individual self (jiva) which shows up as a different presence, is generally (atman) part and appearance of the entire (Brahman).

Despite the fact that there are numerous Mahavakyas, four of them, one from every one of the four Vedas, are regularly referenced as "the Mahavakyas". According to the Vedanta-custom, the topic and the substance of all Upanishads are the equivalents, and all the Upanishadic Mahavakyas express this one widespread message as pithy and compact statements.[citation needed] In later Sanskrit use, the term mahāvākya came to signify "talk", and explicitly, talk on a rationally grandiose topic.

As per the Advaita Vedanta convention, the four Upanishadic articulations show definitive solidarity of the individual (Atman) with Supreme (Brahman).

At the outset, this world was only a solitary body (ātman) formed like a man. He glanced around and saw only himself. The main thing he said was, 'Here I am!' and from that, the name 'I' appeared. [1.4.9] Now, the inquiry is raised; 'Since individuals believe that they will end up being the Whole by knowing Brahma, what did brahman realize that empowered it to turn into the Whole? [1.4.10] before all else, this world was just brahman, and it knew just itself (ātman), thinking: 'I'm Brahma.' thus, it turned into the Whole [...] If a man knows 'I'm brahman along these lines, he turns into the entire world. Not even the divine beings can forestall it, for he turns into their actual self (ātman).

Ahaṁ Brahmāsmi at that point signifies "I'm the Absolute" or "My personality is astronomical," however can likewise be deciphered as "you are essential for god simply like some other component."

In his remark on this section Sankara clarifies that here Brahman isn't the molded Brahman (saguna); that a momentary element can't be interminable; that information about Brahman, the limitless all-infesting substance, has been ordered; that information on non-duality alone scatters obliviousness;

and that the reflection dependent on likeness is just a thought. He additionally reveals to us that the articulation of Aham Brahmaasmi is the clarification of the mantra

That ('Brahman') is boundless, and this ('universe') is endless; the limitless continues from the endless. (At that point) taking the limitlessness of the endless ('universe'), it stays as the endless ('Brahman') alone. - (Brihadaranyaka Upanishad V.i.1)

He clarifies that non-duality and majority are conflicting just when applied to the Self, which is everlasting and without parts, however not with the impacts, which have parts. The aham in this noteworthy articulation isn't shut in itself as an unadulterated mental reflection yet it is extremist transparency. Among Brahman and aham-Brahma lies the whole worldly universe experienced by the uninformed as a different element (duality).

Vidyāranya in his Panchadasi (V.4) clarifies: {{talkquote|Infinite ordinarily, the Supreme Self is portrayed here by the word Brahman (lit. consistently extending; a definitive reality); the word asmi indicates the character of aham and Brahman. Thusly, (the significance of the articulation is) "I'm Brahman."

Vaishnavas, when they talk about Brahman, typically allude to generic Brahman, brahmajyoti (beams of Brahman). Brahman as indicated by them implies God - Narayana, Rama, or Krishna. In this way, the significance of "aham Brahma Asmi" as per their way of thinking is that "I am a drop of Ocean of Consciousness.", or "I'm soul, part of the inestimable soul who is the ultimate Parabrahma". Here, the term Parabrahma is acquainted with keep away from disarray. In the event that Brahman can mean soul (however, Parabrahma is additionally the spirit, yet Supreme one - Paramatma), at that point, Parabrahma ought to allude to God, Lord Vishnu, or whichever deity that one may want to associate with.

In short, it means that this Jeeva Atma indeed is the Brahma that thy holiness has projected with the sole objective to help us realize that we all are equal to God's and thus can elevate each other with the sole realization of our own capabilities with complete and single most dedication on him who is formless and the supreme being.

He who is not seen or reached with severe austerities can easily be achieved by realization of the simple thought of this Mahavakya. So this humble writing that I hope to write is dedicated to him and his teaching with the hope that I can simplify what I understand of his grace and how you too can achieve the same peace I felt since I achieved this realization. He who is above Maaya is indeed achievable and responds readily to those who have faith in him or trust blindly in him while forgoing all their earlier understandings, wants, beliefs, and impure thoughts if there may any.

2

When and how, did I come to this realization?

The year, 2020, was not good for most of us but it was really special for me in ways more than 1. They say that one only seeks for the GOD when in trouble and boy was I in 1. It was like someone had given the address to my house on international trouble station as I went from 1 trouble to another each one breaking myself down till no shame or ego or confidence was left in me. Just two days after my birthday, I was unceremoniously furloughed off. It was not just hard but practically impossible for me to find a job for a very long time, but it is when you lose self do you find the real hope in the form of the one and only. My soul was given to me by 'Shri Guru Charitra' which seemed to be holding the answers to all my questions and the path that I sought to find from within. 'Shri Guru' as I have found to lovingly call him these days is the guide that I am happy to find in these tough times that I still try to evade. For the one who has the support or blessings of his guru shall always be able to find shore in the deepest of oceans and he is known to be holding all his disciples to ensure none of us ever loses sight of our goals.

He taught me that in a nutshell, this whole world that he is running is nothing more than clockwork wherein somewhere someone would do a single simple deed which would give or take something from someone here as though it was planned well before. The funniest part of this is that if he thinks to give something to someone irrespective of the conditions someone somewhere would be working double the effort to ensure it reaches you as though it were magic! Magic it is indeed! His magic is beyond my comprehension or my ability to comprehend too as I am a mere author who cannot even plan the next second without hoping to have his guidance these days. Sorry but the person who evidently losses self in his guru and their teachings only shall be able to find him everywhere. Quite honestly I still fail to comprehend his presence in the current time but I know he is still here and is still able to support and protect me in his own unique way as I am just trusting blindly in him to help me wade away from all my troubles and personal scruples.

What this lockdown personally meant for me and my learnings from this time:

The Covid infection (COVID-19) pandemic is of a scale a great many people alive today have never seen. Lockdowns and curfews to contain the spread of the infection affected the manner in which youngsters learn, the manner in which their families make money, and how safe they feel in their homes and networks. Regardless of the progressing danger, nations around the planet are beginning to lift limitations. As we question whether we will at any point return to what we once knew to be "typical", its value returned a stage to perceive how we can expand on what we have figured out how to work back a superior world for kids.

"I understood that regardless of how long we think we have; by the day's end, what I came to appreciate was that we basically don't invest sufficient quality energy with our families,"

Days in lockdown were a chance for youngsters to rehash methods of play and picking up, investigating their prompt climate and capitalizing on what they had accessible. Building versatility in youngsters is one way we assist them with adapting in troublesome minutes.

Curfews were likewise an opportunity to assist kids with learning obligation and their part in contributing in our own particular manner to discover an answer for aggregate issues. "The quiet comprehension of my youngsters was basically surprising. We remain at home, no inquiries posed, no requests to proceed to play with companions. Their lives have totally changed, yet they appear to get a handle on the significance of their commitment better than most grown-ups,".

During curfews, many found out about the significance of being imaginative with the scant assets and restricted actual space they had at home. Additionally, many came to value that little thoughtful gestures and appreciation to other relatives assist with boosting passionate prosperity.

Some even mastered new abilities yet the thing that matters most is figuring out how to value the passionate associations made between various ages. It's these associations that assist us with building up the enthusiastic versatility we need to overcome unpleasant occasions.

"It is valid – this emergency has negatively affected mankind. Nonetheless, it additionally gave a chance to ages to join together and maybe started to shape our more youthful ages to contemplate their own individual jobs and how we as people would all be able to contribute in our own particular manner to discover an answer for aggregate issues,"

3

If I am Brahma, then what went wrong with 2020?

On the off chance that what you're doing isn't working, you need to address course — not twofold down on the equivalent losing strategy. That has been the situation for quite a while with the U.S. endeavors to contain Covid-19.

Over the most recent few weeks, I've requested a number from specialists what they realize since they wish they'd known in the spring, and where they think general wellbeing misunderstood things. Two major patterns arose: lockdowns (excessively gruff) and testing (excessively lethargic). With months left to go before immunization can diminish the pandemic, 2020's disappointments ought to be 2021's exercises.

College of Minnesota disease transmission expert Michael Osterholm, an individual from Biden's warning board, said one March botch was shutting organizations in places in the country that had seen basically no cases. "Was it fitting to close down such countless things in those days when there was nearly nothing if any transmission? I figure you can contend now that likely was not the best utilization of assets ... it plainly distanced the very populaces that we expected to have work with us," he says.

The time was wasted as was public trust. He thinks about the circumstance of tropical storm alerts. Individuals treat them appropriately because they are normally correct. In numerous Midwest states, individuals went into crisis mode at some unacceptable time.

The previous spring's methodology left the public loaded with malevolence and profoundly isolated, for certain considering the to be as oppressive and others persuaded, similarly as wrongly, that if individuals weren't "self-centered" the control measures would have annihilated the infection. That is never been achievable in a country where such countless individuals reside in jam-packed lodging and can't bear to remain at home.

Hazard correspondence specialist Peter Sandman had it right the previous summer when he said any approach individuals don't follow is an awful strategy. Although control methodologies matter as much as could be expected, because it could require a long time before an antibody consigns this emergency to history, legislators and general wellbeing authorities have wasted individuals' eagerness and capacity to remain at home.

Last April, general wellbeing specialists perceived that lockdowns were never going to destroy the infection from the U.S. When medical clinics were not, at this point at risk for being overpowered, they contended that the reason for proceeding to confine organizations and schools was to delay to get a decent testing technique set up. Yet, that didn't occur.

Harvard disease transmission expert Michael Mina's appraisal of our testing program is condemning. "We're getting basically no viability from a general wellbeing point of view," he says. "Our contact following and testing program is fizzling before our eyes."

Testing is his skill — he's prepared as a pathologist and directs diagnostics at Brigham and Women's Hospital in Boston. Coronavirus tests work for diagnosing individuals who get amazingly sick, yet they aren't appropriate to discovering contaminated individuals before they send the infection.

"This infection has an exceptionally intense window — a short window when individuals can spread," he says. The individuals who get a positive outcome back are likely past their most infectious period, and those with a negative outcome may not actually be negative on the off chance that they don't get the outcomes back for quite a long time.

The more lawmakers and the media support testing, the more individuals line up for them, the more drawn out the outcomes take and the less helpful they become. Labs are overpowered with swabs, Mina says, thus they sit for quite a long time. He says it would be better for labs to decline to take swabs on the off chance that they can't deal with them in 24 hours. Better to deal with a large portion of the examples in a noteworthy time window than none of them.

"There's no motivation to put a swab in somebody's nose if how we're doing the outcomes isn't valuable any longer," he says. Modest home tests that require minutes would help, and they are really being fabricated quicker than individuals are utilizing them, he says, since general wellbeing hasn't spread out a procedure for them.

Mina stresses that we're not getting a usable testing procedure because there's a background marked by paternalism in general wellbeing. There's a demeanor that on the off chance that we enabled individuals to discover their status, they would go out and party. The same thing occurred with at-home pregnancy tests, he said, with general wellbeing authorities at first not confiding in ladies to utilize them effectively.

He has upheld ordinary testing — in any event once and ideally double seven days with simple, quick tests, as certain schools have done to keep cases low. Besides, testing is something individuals need, he says. They need to know their status considerably more than they need to wear veils or maintain a strategic distance from others.

A more astute way to deal with testing and lockdowns would go far toward saving lives — and making 2021 more tolerable than 2020.

After burning through many hours in 2020 conversing with specialists, I've left away perceiving that they don't have the foggiest idea how to control a Covid pandemic — that they're making suggestions as they come. That is everything anybody can manage, as long as they quit rehashing similar mix-ups.

4

If I am Brahma, then what is wrong with 2021?

This previous year, 2020 was something beyond a marker of where we existed on schedule—it was fundamentally its own demeanor. Between the pandemic, police ruthlessness and other brutality against Black individuals, and turbulent political race that characterized the year, 2020 got shorthand for death, tension, outrage, trouble, anguish, injury, forlornness, and torment. At the point when individuals asked us how we were doing, we could reply, "All things considered, you know, it's 2020." When something terrible occurred, we said, "That is 2020 for you." I sincerely can't tally the number of images, tweets, and jokes with zingers that added up to, "So…2020, am I right?" These previous few months particularly, 2020 was something we simply needed to be finished.

All things considered, here we are. It's 2021. On the off chance that everything went by our end-all strategy, the entirety of our issues ought to be gone and all ought to be great now, correct? Prompt the birds and monstrous Roaring Twenties–like gatherings that everybody says we ought to have when the pandemic is finished.

No doubt, I wish. Truth be told, with the new upset endeavor in Washington,

D.C., neglect trusting that 2021 will be superior to 2020—now, a ton of us are as of now trusting it just will not be more terrible. It just required six days to arrive at the top 2020 degrees of enthusiastic depletion. Six.

OK, consistently, the greater part of us realized that nothing would mystically change because 2020 finished. We realized that the scheduled year exchanging or the ball dropping wouldn't in a flash stamp the finish of this injury and misfortune.

Furthermore, yet...aren't you somewhat let down at any rate? Didn't you sort of wish, where it counts, that you'd be refuted? No doubt, many individuals are feeling that way. It's a thing. Furthermore, it's befuddling. How could so many of us, despite realizing better, actually feel baffled that entering 2021 didn't accompany even a LITTLE alleviation?

Indeed, there are a couple of reasons. For one, trusting things would improve in 2021, even unknowingly, was a significant method for dealing with stress for some this previous year. It happens normally when things feel so crazy and questionable. Zeroing in on a characterized timeframe or a particular wellspring of our torment—say, 2020—permitted us to make a little request in the turmoil. You didn't really need to accept that this hellscape had an unmistakable start and end for that to be valid. The desire for it was sufficient. Consider having a youngster in their horrible twos—definitely, their third birthday celebration is absolutely subjective, yet don't you sort of let yourself trust they'll begin outgrowing their fits when it shows up?

With the goal that setback we feel? That is a blend of our squashed expectation and the acknowledgment (or affirmation) that this is every one of the significantly less brief than we needed it to be. Depleted and genuinely depleted, we crept through the finish of 2020 as the finish of a long-distance race, simply needing to cross the end goal, get our inept cooperation prize and silver space cover, and pledge never to do it again in our lives. Yet, we didn't get that. There were no murmurs of alleviation and time for recuperation. All things being equal, we need to continue onward, continue attempting, and continue to endure.

We actually don't know for how long. The end goal continues to move. At the point when the primary immunizations opened up, for example, a great deal of us felt an immense liberating sensation thus much expectation that we moved in the roads. However, the numerous issues with the rollout have just taken us back to our typical fear and disappointment. The desire for a finish to this, once more, got pushed back. What's more, who can say for sure when we'll have a distantly broadened quiet period strategically, given ongoing occasions.

The previous few months we were so centered around enduring 2020 that now that we're here, it's sort of like, "Okay...what next?" Is the new benchmark "getting past 2021"? Since supposing that anyway, how overpowering is that? It's no big surprise 2021 has effectively left us feeling let down and depleted and terrified and pitiful.

All that said, because these sentiments are totally typical doesn't mean they're not difficult to manage. So as psychological wellness was proficient, I needed to suggest two things you can do right presently to deal with yourself.

Above all else, cut yourself a little room to breathe. Regardless of whether you came into this realizing it wouldn't feel good and are pounding yourself for feeling disillusioned in any case, or you accepted you'd feel much improved and now feel guileless, you were just adapting all that could be expected. Have some self-sympathy. On the off chance that the occasions of this current week have just aggravated this for you, set aside an effort to do some self-care in the manner that works for you.

I likewise prescribe setting aside some effort to deliberately ponder 2020 somehow or another. I realize you may be enticed to put it behind you and never reconsider it, yet reflection is significant and may even facilitate a portion of the hurt you're feeling. In injury treatment, we have individuals recount their story, recorded as a hard copy or so anyone can hear, because it assists them with controlling the account. We now and again say on the off chance that you can expound on it, you are not, at this point caught by it. And keeping in mind that a significant number of the injuries of 2020 haven't passed and a portion of the injuries of 2021 is now adding to them, you actually endure such a lot a year ago and that merits checking. Communicating it will help you continue so you can keep on enduring. On the off chance that we skirt crafted by preparing our feelings and encounters, every last bit of it will eventually surface more seriously than previously.

You can consider the great, the awful, and the revolting. You can note what 2020 resembled for you, what you realized, what you cherished, what you missed, and what you felt. You may add how you feel changed constantly because it is difficult to envision that you don't. You can decide to never impart it to anybody, or decide to impart it to whoever you need that feels like a protected individual to tell.

You may find that doing this gives that sensation of progress that you were expecting, regardless of little, so you can push ahead into 2021 feeling like you've left probably a portion of the load behind you. It may even give you a perspective on occasions of this previous week with a smidgen more point of view, security, and establishing.

Furthermore, recollect: You don't need to—and shouldn't—abandon trust that things will improve, regardless of whether you feel disillusioned or senseless at this point. The expectation is never something senseless. Truth be told, it is very an excellent one.

5

How can one realize the same?

This realization or feeling I achieved was with the grace of his true self only, like a person who gets the support of a log, I got this book/ feeling/ realization with his divine grace. The funny thing is that I still don't think that I have anyway done or am doing something different or outstanding that he seems to be responding to me by answering all my questions and apprehensions once they raise their ugly head. It is he who reached out it seems in my case to help me cross these tough times and help me realize his grace.

Realization of who he is and how he can help can only be achieved through a guru or a person who is above joy & sorrow, one with him and one who can transcend the duality of Maaya to show us the right path of self-discovery. For me, this happened through the grace of SREEMATH HARIHARAPURA's SRIMAJJAGADGURU SHANKARACHARYA SRI SRI SWAYAMPRAKASHA SACHI-DANANDA SARASWATHI MAHASWAMIJI, whom I visited unconsciously through the good faith of my Dad who had learned of his presence in some way. He helped and continues to help me even though I seemed to have given him nothing in return yet.

His grace is such that a true guru without expecting nothing in return saves his disciples that he has accepted and helps them through self-realization of the right path. My single visit to this place has helped me achieve such grace that he continues to still guide me to the path of righteousness and ensure that through one form or the other I continue to get his Prasada to ensure to be on the right path. He has in all honesty robbed me of my despair and shone like a million suns to grace me like the billions of moons with peace of mind and coolness to be able to walk on the right path even in the toughest of times.

With his grace, I have never felt alone or lost as with his simple thought he invokes in me the trust that there is he who is listening and providing me with all that I may need at each turn of my life. All that I need to do is continue walking the path of realization and do good which I can do for the rest he is always there to help.

So, I say find your guru, your true inspiration, your solace in this Maaya driven world for he alone can help you cross this ocean with his support & grace, one can unlock the true mysteries of life and find the ultimate truth to become one with him who protects, graces, supports and sustains us. But do remember that total and complete surrender to him for the slightest doubt in his teachings or words may be the cause of losing his grace and getting lost in this world again. Rise with his grace and become one with him. May you all find his grace and experience his grace that I have begun feeling since having been in his presence.

6

Why can't I myself come to this realization?

"**M**y reality on this planet is futile."

That idea entered my thoughts consistently before I nodded off.

It had been a while since I moved on from secondary school and I had no clue about how I planned to manage my life. My tentative arrangements were self-destructing, and everybody around me continued disclosing to me that I expected to begin getting things done that I had not at this point achieved.

I was not where I figured I ought to be throughout everyday life. Everybody had assumptions that I hadn't met. I turned out to be too centered around turning into a variant of myself that every other person needed, and I continually contrasted myself with others who had effectively brought the jump into the following section of their life.

I was determinedly addressed and decided for my more slow movement throughout everyday life, which persuaded me that nobody upheld me or had faith in me. I asked why I even tried to exist on the off chance that I was wasting time and disillusioning everybody. I started to reprimand everybody except myself for the mindset of hopelessness I had fallen into.

My confidence started to endure as the months passed by. I felt the second rate compared to everybody and it made me disdain myself. I actually didn't have the foggiest idea how I needed to manage my life—and I was beginning to not give it a second thought.

Be that as it may, a while and many unnecessary self put-downs later, I chose to shut out the antagonism, both from myself and others. I quieted the voice in my mind that disclosed to me I wasn't sufficient and asked myself what might truly satisfy me.

I've generally been innovative and expressive. I used to sing, act, and dance when I was more youthful. However, my number one thing has consistently been composing.

The absolute most joyful minutes in my day-to-day existence came from freedoms to communicate or put my central core out for anyone's viewing pleasure. Each way I attempted to return consistently drove me to compose.

I arrived at a point where I understood that I was simply attempting to seek after different ways since I imagined that is the thing that others would acknowledge. I was anxious about the possibility that if I let my creative mind take off to every one of the various prospects, individuals would destroy me or advise me to be "practical."

Most importantly I got deadened with this dread of not being acknowledged. I was hesitant to appear as something else or head out in a different direction and seek after what genuinely satisfied me. I put myself in a case.

At some point, I concluded that enough was sufficient. I spent a whole year of my life attempting to be "sensible" and adjust to the assumptions of others. I understood that you can't satisfy everybody, at any rate, so trying will not prompt happiness.

Genuine joy comes from being content with and glad for yourself.

I at long last concluded that I planned to give my chance to finding out about composition and dealing with my composing abilities. I'm content with that choice and I rest easy thinking about myself since I made it for myself.

I have taken in a couple of things about picking the correct way for yourself, zeroing in on what will satisfy you. On the off chance that you've been battling to settle on that decision, I suggest:

Drop your concerns.

Stress puts the weight at the forefront of your thoughts, body, and soul. They can keep you up throughout the evening on the off chance that you let them. Discover comfort in the way that everything occurs for an explanation and all that will become alright at the correct time.

During my time of low confidence and outrageous vulnerability, I tirelessly scrutinized each part of my life. I would hit the hay baffled and agitated as I revealed to myself I wasn't sufficient, and that I wanted to resemble every other person my age.

By continually slamming yourself and agonizing over each and everything that happens to you, you're passing up bliss that you could've had from the start.

Try not to attempt to please or intrigue anybody however yourself.

The need to intrigue, please, and contrast ourselves with others all the time is perhaps the most widely recognized reason for self-hatred. However long you're attempting to satisfy others and satisfy their hopes, you won't be satisfying yourself.

What I've discovered is that joy doesn't come from satisfying others. Bliss comes from feeling content with your own life and objectives.

Embrace your exceptional characteristics and gifts.

Everybody is extraordinary. Sort out what you're acceptable at and what separates you from every other person. Your central goal is to make a just being here.

Put stock in your way.

At the point when you begin to sort out what you need throughout everyday life, there will be obstructions. Try not to let any person or thing deter you from forging ahead. Trust in yourself and have confidence in your choices.

Stay positive and continue to push ahead.

Take as much time as is needed.

Life doesn't accompany a rulebook or cutoff times for getting certain things done. I used to consistently feel that I should have been at a similar level as every other person my age. Life isn't a race or a challenge.

Have confidence in the way that you are by and large where you should be at present on schedule and insofar as you're content, don't allow anybody to persuade you that you're not where you should be. You be the adjudicator of what you need to change in your life and afterward do it for you.

Encircle yourself with inspiration.

Attempt to restrict the measure of time you go through with individuals who nay-say, judge, or criticism. Decide to totally encircle yourself with positive, moving impacts. You will feel a lot more joyful and better about yourself if you do.

Make a rundown of idioms or statements that cause you to feel supported or motivated and keep it where you can see it every day. Have a go at putting the rundown under your pad or on your cooler entryway.

The main thing to recollect is that you are awesome, you can go one more day, and you can be cheerful. Life won't toss you anything you can't deal with or survive.

When you begin to acknowledge and adore yourself and your ideal way, the air will clear and you will inhale simple once more. Be caring to yourself and life will be a ton more splendid.

7

How can this realization take away all expectations and sorrow?

O dds are, you're occupied with hustling between the 40 hours per week you need to work, the family you need to accommodate, and the bills that should be paid.

As the years cruise by, you've started to feel the burnout from every one of the necessities and assumptions expected of you. You don't feel like you are in charge of your own life. Indeed, it seems like the conditions in your day-to-day existence are controlling you.

Imagine a scenario in which there was a path for you to have the option to have better control of your life and make every one of the positive changes you've been throbbing for.

This should be possible through self-acknowledgment.

You've likely known about this idea previously, yet you're not entirely certain what it truly is or how it can help you.

I will jump into what precisely self-acknowledgment is and the specific advances you can take to accomplish it for yourself. Peruse on the off chance that you need to figure out how to open your latent capacity and figure out how to diminish your pressure and nervousness, and gain completely clear clearness about what your identity is and what you're able to do.

What Is Self-Realization?

Self-acknowledgment has a couple of large definitions. In the Western world, it's by and large characterized as the initiation of one's maximum capacity of gifts and capacities.

How Psychologists Define Self-Realization

Humanistic brain research additionally follows a comparative line of reasoning about self-acknowledgment.

Clinician Abraham Maslow has named individuals he considered to have arrived at self-acknowledgment like Albert Einstein, Abraham Lincoln, and Eleanor Roosevelt to give some examples. His renowned chain of importance of requirements hypothesis states to accomplish self-acknowledgment (or for this situation, Maslow utilizes the expression "self-actualization"),[1] one necessity to have a specific arrangement of requirements met before accomplishing it:[2]

For instance, self-acknowledgment can't be accomplished if you are battling monetarily and too made up for the lost time in agonizing over how to pay for the lease and give food to your family. Shockingly, this is generally the situation for some individuals, which leaves little freedom for them to augment their capacities.

How Religions Define Self-Realization

In religions, the idea of self-acknowledgment is taken from an alternate point of view through and through. Associating with your most genuine self has a ton to would with rising above your own care and body. This self is regularly considered as an unceasing being that isn't kept to the actual space that your brain and body take up. Many perceive this piece of yourself as the spirit.

To put these definitions together, self-acknowledgment is at last learning the response to the fundamental question, "Who am I?"

The appropriate response lies in understanding that you are not your feelings or your musings. Who you truly are isn't even your body or your psyche. These are everything you as a self encounter, however, they are not you.

Furthermore, when you are too up to speed in these things that are not yours, that is the point at which you succumb to and stall out in your negative encounters like pressure, uneasiness, and dread.

While your considerations, emotions, and actual body consistently transform, you don't.

I realize this idea can be somewhat confounding to see, so here's an extraordinary video that investigates who you truly are clarified by Prince EA.

Why Self-Realization Matters to You

How regularly would you say you are diverted, lost in your contemplations, or overpowered by troublesome feelings?

Being in the present is more troublesome than any time in recent memory with the innovation today. Individuals are frequently covered in their cell phones or workstations while others around are desiring their consideration.

The vast majority invest so little energy in the present. They're generally either harmed and experiencing difficulty relinquishing their past, or caught up with stressing over their fates:

Here are some astonishing advantages to self-acknowledgment:

The capacity to screen your feelings. Maybe then being constrained by your feelings, you would now be able to utilize your perceptions about them during the experience to figure out how to adequately deal with things like dread, uneasiness, and stress. Self-acknowledge assists you with doing this by giving you the expertise of relinquishing crippling emotions and grabbing hold of the enabling ones all things considered.

Improved concentration and focus. Guided by your own internal objectives and qualities, self-acknowledgment assists you with recognizing when you are going into interruptions and dispose of them. By disposing of the insignificant things in your day-to-day existence, you stay focused on what makes a difference most and you start to consider genuine to be as you arrive at your fullest potential.

Expanded certainty, mindfulness, and confidence. By being associated profoundly with your most genuine self, self-acknowledgment liberates you from any frailties, stresses, and low self-appreciation worth that you grope tangled in by assisting you with getting a handle on the reality that you are not characterized by them.

Getting more tolerating of yourself and others. You can be more real and express feelings unreservedly and unmistakably. Thus, you can frame further connections and invest more energy interfacing with individuals as opposed to attempting to dazzle them.

At the point when individuals don't have their very own solid feeling self, they get handily influenced to carry on with life how others advise them to live it.

The reality of this has appeared through Bronnie Ware's well-known work, which has shown that one of the top second thoughts of individuals who are kicking the bucket was:

There can be huge loads of pressing factors whether it's from work, society, and even loved ones for you to be a sure way. Possibly your harsh childhood ingrained a solid requirement for other's endorsement in you so you do what others expect of you. Perhaps you've quit confiding in individuals because of your battles with relinquishing the considerations and encounters that hurt you.

Whatever the circumstance, self-acknowledgment gives you the protected space you need to mend and develop.

The most effective method to Start Developing Self-Realization

1. Begin Meditating Regularly

Besides all the logical proof that shows the medical advantages of contemplation, it is additionally a superb method to accomplish self-acknowledgment.

One of my most loved applications that control you through reflection is Headspace.

I especially love this application since it is clear without all the charm kinds of things you typically partner with reflection. It works effectively in demystifying what reflection truly is and how it can profit you from accomplishing self-acknowledgment.

You can get the fundamental contemplation direction for nothing or pay for a superior adaptation for admittance to more explicit reflections that improve things such as confidence, innovativeness, and connections.

If you would prefer not to download the application, here is the basic reflection practice you can do at present:

Sit serenely on a seat.

Start by leaving your eyes open with a casual delicate core interest.

Require about a moment to take full breaths in through your nose and out through your mouth.

After a couple of full breaths, tenderly close your eyes while you are breathing out.

Resume typical relaxing.

Pause for a minute to stop and appreciate being available at the time with having nothing to do, no place to go, nothing to check.

Pause for a minute to feel the pressing factor of your body on the seat underneath you, the feet on the floor and the hands and the arms simply laying on the legs.

Tenderly take the concentration back to your relaxing.

As you stay there seeing the breath and the body with its rising and falling sensation, don't attempt to stop your considerations. Essentially permit them to simply go back and forth.

Now, the lone thing you need to do is the point at which you've understood your psyche has meandered, delicately take the concentration back to your breath once more.

Delicately take the consideration back to your body, back to that sensation of contact to your seat and the space around you and when prepared, tenderly open your eyes once more.

Regardless of whether it's just 5-10 minutes every day, figuring out how to prepare your brain to be available is so essential to your excursion towards self-acknowledgment. You need to make a stride back from the insanity of life and recompose yourself to be available for the things that matter most.

Another incredible technique that can be utilized to accomplish self-acknowledgment that includes somewhat more body strength is yoga. While there are numerous varieties of yoga and has likewise become an extremely well-known type of activity in western culture, its unique reason filled in as a thoughtful practice to accomplish the more elevated level of cognizance that comes from self-acknowledgment.

You can get to a lot of free Yoga channels on Youtube or join an exercise center to begin.

2. Set aside a few minutes for Self-Realization Every Day

I understand your're's opinion.

"I don't possess energy for this!"

I tend to disagree.

Around 40% of the things you do in a day don't include effectively settling on a choice. All things considered, it is really a propensity.

Out of the entirety of your propensities, there are likely a modest bunch of terrible ones. On the off chance that you can notice your everyday schedules, there is a straightforward method to change a negative behavior pattern into a decent one, which is to begin making changes to your current circumstance to make it simpler for you to change your propensities.

The thought is as opposed to attempting to crush in more opportunity to accomplish something, essentially adjust an everyday propensity you have into something different.

For instance, suppose you start your morning by fermenting your espresso and plunking down on the eating table for 20 minutes to peruse the web to get up to speed with the news.

The news is normally brimming with negative data, so why not go through those 20 minutes in contemplation all things considered?

One simple approach to roll out this improvement is to switch your current circumstance up by keeping your PC and telephone in an alternate room so you don't have quick admittance to it when you plunk down on the feasting table. You make it simpler on yourself to invest energy pondering as opposed to gazing at a screen.

Need some more extraordinary tips on bringing an end to negative behavior patterns? You can evaluate Lifehack CEO's mysterious Control Alternate Delete technique, which was the strategy he used to bring an end to 3 unfortunate propensities in under 2 months.

Last Thoughts

Self-acknowledgment doesn't occur incidentally. It will require some investment and practice, however, if you transform the practices into a propensity, you'll be ensured to arrive. When you do, you'll at last feel like you are in more command over your life and have the option to get yourself to the following level.

8

How can this realization make anyone feel void of suffering?

In the phase of Pure Consciousness, we may pose a similar inquiry we asked in the Void stage. "When everything is gone, what stays?" In the Void stage, we previously replied, "Nothing." until we gradually acknowledged what is consistently here. At the point when we understood that Consciousness is consistently here and without it, we were unable to know about the Void stage, we understood something different, something significant, something earth-changing, something that totally breaks the individual self, all accounts, all insights, everything. Cognizance is consistently here. And surprisingly more awe-inspiring, nothing else is. Just Consciousness exists.

Call it Consciousness, Awareness, the Absolute, Brahman, God, the Source, the Creator, or whatever name you pick. Nothing exists except for This. Furthermore, since nothing can exist except for This, you are This.

All that you see, taste, feel, contact, smell, think, or feel is just This. What's more, the one seeing, tasting, feeling, contacting, smelling, thinking and feeling, is just This. There is totally taking all things together of presence only This. What a colossally significant revelation. Intellectually, you can't move toward this. How should you? For what reason would you? Your considerations are made in duality, the confidence in the division. Your contemplations are articulations of duality. The acknowledgment of This breaks all musings. This immediate acknowledgment comes from somewhere else. It is past contemplations and past sentiments. It is past the scholar, the antenna, and the experiencer. But it is really and Absolutely what you are.

When totally all the other things are gone, This is here, shinning in its totally brilliant brilliance. Furthermore, you are It.

Musings can't envision this. They can't approach. Try not to try and attempt. You will just make a fantasy out of Ultimate Truth.

At the point when this acknowledgment turns out to be genuine, when you have sunk profoundly into it, glance around. Take a gander at your hand. It is God, wonderful past any idea of excellence. Get your number one book of nature photos or take a gander at a wonderful photo of nightfall or mountain on the Internet. There is just God, just Brahman, just the Absolute, just Consciousness Itself. Also, the Absolute is the lone thing looking. No place altogether presence is there anything besides This.

Take a gander at your dearest companion, your better half, or an outsider in the city. It's all God. There isn't anything else. That it is so stunning too, at last, understand this. You don't need to say anything. I wouldn't on the off chance that I was you. Hardly any individuals can comprehend what you have quite recently experienced.

Understand that even this is simply one more story. In any case, this is an exceptionally significant level story. This story obliterates any remaining stories. In the case of everything is God, what else would you be able to say about a tree, an individual, the world, yourself? Any remaining stories vanish in the brilliance of this changing story. Living in acknowledgment of this story, you live in the Bliss of the Absolute. In the end, you let go of even this last story as well and live with no accounts by any means. You are free, totally free. Everything is basically what it is without a story to shroud its extraordinary brilliance.

Contemplation/Samadhi

At this point, contemplation has changed to Samadhi. It isn't a normal thing for you. It's totally easy. You just fall into it, such as falling in reverse into limitless space. You are invested in the Absolute. Like emptying some water into the endless sea, the water is totally invested in the sea and no longer has any character separate from the sea Itself. Because of the huge Bliss and Freedom, you end up investing increasingly more energy here. Each extra second, you fall into Samadhi. When you and the world have vanished, what else would you be able to do? What else bodes well?

The outright Bliss of Samadhi maneuvers you into it like gravity pulls your body when you are falling. You don't attempt to enter Samadhi, you just fall into it. It applies its own incredible and powerful power. You basically don't avoid it. You can't avoid it.

You may consider Samadhi complete assimilation in the Divine or God. You don't understand just yourself as God and separate from whatever else, all that isn't God. Everything is God. There is basically nothing that isn't God. God is everything that matters. God is all that exists.

In Samadhi, the world and self as we have realized them vanish. This isn't so not the same as what occurs in the Void. In any case, here the Something Else isn't Emptiness or Void. It is difficult to portray or make an idea around. It is All That Exists and all that exists is just It. Any word you use to portray it can't be It. All words vanish Here. All musings vanish Here. The world and oneself vanish Here. All that remains is this Infinite Absolute Self.

The Three Levels of Samadhi

In conventional writing, three degrees of Samadhi are depicted.

1. Savikalpa Samadhi

In the principal level of Samadhi, the meditator has not yet totally lost the differentiation between the experiencer, the experience, and what is capable. The principal level actually includes some exertion. However, not at all like what is capable when you start pondering. On the off chance that any contemplations emerge, basically ask would could it be that knows about that idea. In this manner, you may keep the consideration zeroed in on mindfulness Itself. Whatever emerges in the psyche, disregard it and get back to what exactly knows about the idea or experience. You are not, at this point inspired by the object of reflection, however the subject and what is past the subject, what knows about the subject.

In this phase of reflection, you will encounter minutes, minutes, and even hours when all duality, both you and the world, vanish altogether. This is joined by extraordinary rapture. In any case, ultimately, you will get back to your more conventional cognizance. Savikalpa Samadhi is frequently knowledgeable about the Pure Being/Bliss condition of cognizance.

As you experience this opportunity and ecstasy all the more often and for longer timeframes, you will normally move to a more profound degree of Samadhi called Nirvikalpa Samadhi.

2. Nirvikalpa Samadhi

Here all considerations have stopped and you are completely caught up in the Absolute. There could be not, at this point any differentiation between experiencer, experience, and what is capable. Duality has finished. Assimilation is finished and nothing upsets it or occupies from it. Drenched in an expanse of Bliss, every interior article (considerations) and outer items (the world) have vanished. This is an easy condition of reflection. It resembles gravity to a falling body. You are maneuvered into it by a powerful power. Nirvikalpa Samadhi is the regular reflection province of Pure Consciousness/Oneness. It is existence without a story.

Mix

At the outset, emerging from this profundity of contemplation can be somewhat difficult. For one thing, there is no craving to. For what reason would you need to leave a maritime condition of rapture? It resembles in Near-Death encounters when the Light is entered. No one needs to return. Be that as it may, something of the world typically pulls you back. At that point, there is the test of re-arranging and coordinating. What you have encountered is so absolutely dissimilar to anything you have at any point experienced previously. The world appears to be totally stunning. Everything is both God but then various appearances show up simultaneously. Be that as it may, those appearances appear to be absolutely unbelievable, as though you are taking a gander at a fantasy realizing it is a fantasy. It requires some investment to sink into this experience. Your capacity to work on the planet may take a little becoming accustomed to also. It is absolutely clear now that all that exists is God/Brahman/Consciousness. Be that as it may, what to think about these different appearances you are presently seeing once more? Similarly, as you fell into this experience with no exertion on your part, the incorporation likewise happens normally with no exertion on your part. Unwind. Try not to stress over it. Allow it to incorporate. Try not to attempt to sort out it. It's all incident impeccably.

3. Sahaja Samadhi

Ramana Maharshi alludes to the total ingestion of Nirvikalpa Samadhi just like a brief condition of retention. He looks at it to a can brought down into a well. While the pail is lowered in the water retention is finished. In any case, there is as yet a rope joined to the can so it tends to be pulled out. With Sahaja Samadhi that rope is no more. There is consistently finished retention. But then it is as yet conceivable to work in a physical and mental world although the experience is totally not quite the same as what a great many people insight.

The development starting with one degree of Samadhi then onto the next comes essentially from investing however much energy as could be expected drenched in these conditions of ingestion. It is a characteristic change. Try not to overemphasize these conditions of ingestion. In any case, permit the acknowledge that emerge to totally saturate and change your life and how you see the world.

In past phases of Consciousness, you may have heard and encountered that everything is a declaration of God, similar to the beams of the sun. There is just one sun, however, there are limitless beams. In this stage, you experience that everything IS God. There are no beams. There are no outflows of God separate from God. It is all God. A piece of God doesn't exist inside each individual. There is no individual. There is ONLY God, just the Absolute, just Infinite Consciousness Itself. So this is an altogether different approach to see the world and the one seeing the world. Everything is God.

Everything Is God

In Sahaja Samadhi you coordinate your experience and acknowledgment in Nirvikalpa Samadhi that everything is God and that the Absolute is all that exists. You bring this experience once again into the universe of duality, structure, and name. You actually see a delightful rainbow in the sky after an evening precipitation shower. In any case, presently the presence of that rainbow, lovely all things considered, is undeniably less significant than the way that you are seeing God. Also, that causes it to feel endlessly more lovely. The downpour, the mists, the mountain, the traffic, a piece of canine crap in the city, and the one seeing this is similarly as wonderful. It's all more endlessly excellent than anything you might have at any point envisioned before this acknowledgment.

You've gotten back home. You've gotten back to the Source you would never have left since that Source is you. Then you felt was you so far is still here. Yet, it is only a fantasy, a deception, an appearance. It holds no interest for you other than how it can communicate this Infinite Absolute Consciousness in a manner others can comprehend. You now carry on with an existence of complete assistance. The possibility of individual or individual edification evaporates totally when you understood undeniably it is all God. Each individual you see is simply God, typically not yet acknowledging Himself. There can be no individual, individual illumination because there is no distinct individual to be edified. There isn't even illumination. There is simply God. That's it in a nutshell. That is It.

You walk delicately on this planet since it is all God. The earth, the walkway, the minuscule insects rushing around, and the one strolling are largely God. None are better or more terrible, more significant or less significant than some other. It's simply God. It's all God. Furthermore, it's a nonstop marvel.

This is how you coordinate this significant acknowledgment, God-Realization, Self-Realization. You are God strolling. You are God seeing. And all God sees is God.

You may approach your life precisely as you had before this significant acknowledgment. Nothing outwardly may seem to change. Indeed, even your dearest companions may just notice that you appear to consistently be cheerful and nothing pesters you. Or then again your life may change an extraordinary arrangement. Assuming that is valid, these progressions likely previously started in before stages. A few groups wind up sitting in a cavern for a very long time. For others, there might be no outer method to perceive any distinction, other than that they generally appear to be grinning. Whatever happens, will occur. It's not, at this point your business. There could be not, at this point you to have a business. There is simply God.

9

AHAAM BRAHMASMI! How can this awaken my confidence, post which one would not need any affirmations?

L ife in the present hyper-associated world is a long way from great. It is not difficult to lose all sense of direction in an ocean of contradictory signals about who you ought to be and what your life ought to resemble.

While some self-improvement ideas might be acceptable, others can be out and out harming.

Besides, you are in all probability attempting to fulfill your requirements and the necessities of people around you. You need to perform well grinding away, have passing marks, or be a decent life partner, parent, or companion. The rundown goes on.

Be that as it may, there is an answer. It's called self-acknowledgment. What's more, it's quite possibly the most integral asset available to you with regards to releasing your maximum capacity.

The True Importance Of Self-Realization

Self-acknowledgment or self-completion is an idea as old as mankind. It has been a piece of every single significant religion and method of reasoning from the beginning of time somehow. It is a significant idea in both eastern and western societies.

Not all characterize it similarly, albeit all have a similar objective at the top of the priority list. That objective is a serene, satisfying life – an existence of ethicalness and plenitude.

Self-acknowledgment can carry endless advantages to the individual who accomplishes it. It influences every one of the twelve everyday issues as characterized in Mindvalley's earth-shattering Lifebook Program made by Jon Butcher. Here are probably the best advantages acknowledgment offers:

1. Higher Confidence And Self-Esteem

People on the way of self-acknowledgment are associated with their internal identities and their general surroundings on a significant level. The profundity and strength of the association can liberate them from stresses, fears, and sensations of shamefulness. Additionally, it allows them to saddle their maximum capacity.

2. A Sharper Focus

The individuals who embrace acknowledgment are in contact with their actual self and work as per their most profound beliefs and qualities. They can characterize their objectives and seek after them with more life and a more honed center. Self-acknowledged individuals rapidly kill harmful impacts from their lives, opening up space for the great stuff.

3. Not Being Controlled By Emotions

Self-acknowledged individuals are not constrained by their feelings. Acknowledgment shows individuals who embrace it how to notice, face, and beat their feelings. Realization shows individuals how to acquire an understanding of their feelings and become proficient at taking care of dread, uneasiness, dejection, and different feelings that keep them down.

4. Acknowledgment

Self-completed people are more open and tolerant than individuals who still can't seem to understand their maximum capacity. They can impart their feelings openly and in a true way. This prompts further and more significant associations with others.

what is self-realization

Understanding The Self-Realization Definition

As an idea, the acknowledgment is available in both eastern and western ways of thinking and religions.

Western culture takes a gander at it from a more logical point of view. Then again, it is profoundly woven into eastern religions like Jainism, Hinduism, Buddhism, and Sikhism.

Anyway, what's simply the definition of acknowledgment?

Among the numerous mental speculations and definitions, the definition by Abraham Maslow is maybe the most generally acknowledged.

Fundamentally, the western meaning of self-acknowledgment is arriving at one's maximum capacity, fulfilling the full extent of one's requirements, and adding to everyone's benefit of humanity or society.

Eastern spiritualities, then again, characterize self-acknowledgment from an alternate point of view.

In Jainism, self-acknowledgment is the expulsion of all counterfeit layers of character and understanding the genuine self and the idea of the real world.

Hinduism characterizes acknowledgment as the information on one's actual self that is a past hallucination and the bounds of the material marvels.

Buddhism sees acknowledgment as an enlivening to the genuine reality.

In Sikhism, the acknowledgment is conceivable through isolating the self from one's own bogus conscience.

What Are Self-Actualization Needs?

Abraham Maslow's meaning of self-completion is defined as looking like a five-level pyramid. Each level of the pyramid addresses one degree of fundamental human necessities. Here are the levels from the most reduced to the most elevated:

Physiological necessities

Security needs

Love and social requirements

Confidence needs

Self-realization

What's the significance here To Be Self-Actualized?

Acting naturally realized methods numerous things. It intends to be in contact with your internal identity and have a full comprehension of your feelings and requirements. Additionally, it implies arriving at your maximum capacity taking all things together everyday issues, and having profound, significant associations with friends and family.

What Is self-completion in Maslow's pecking order of necessities?

As per Maslow's hypothesis, the self-completion stage can just start after the necessities of the past four phases have been met. To act naturally realized is to turn into the most ideal individual. It is to take a stab at your own most prominent advantage and the advantage of others.

self-completion

Would you be able to Reach Self-Actualization?

The short response to this inquiry is: Yes, you can get self-completed. Significant religions and mental speculations all concur that completion is conceivable. The way to accomplish it might change, yet completion is conceivable.

The way to acknowledgment and completion can be a long and troublesome one. This for the most part relies upon your present situation throughout everyday life. Nonetheless, with devotion and difficult work, everything is conceivable.

How To Achieve Actualization?

For the individuals who wish to depend on science, you can have a go at following Maslow's chain of command of requirements. Check what levels you have cleared and what your present level is. Make a move arrangement and make it from that point.

If you need a more otherworldly encounter, you can begin your excursion with contemplation. It has been around for over 3,000 years and it's perhaps the most ideal approach to accomplish realization. Reflection additionally has various medical advantages. Probably the most noticeable include:

Lower feelings of anxiety

Diminished melancholy

Improved rest

Diminished nervousness

Alongside reflection, you can likewise attempt yoga. This centuries-old practice works your body alongside your psyche. Today, yoga is perhaps the most famous type of activity in the west. There are numerous schools and studios out there, so discovering one shouldn't be an issue. Alongside unwinding and exercise, yoga additionally has various other beneficial outcomes.

Last Words

Self-acknowledgment is one of the mainstays of an effective and satisfying life. It will permit you to release your maximum capacity and become the individual you need to be. It will likewise make you more fearless, careful, and centered. Besides, acknowledgment allows you to associate with your internal identity and individuals around you on a significant level.

10

SRIMAJJAGADGURU SHANKARACHARYASRI SRI SWAYAMPRAKASHA SACHIDANANDA SARASWATHI MAHASWAMIJI

Poojyasri Jagadguru Shankaracharya Sri Swayamprakasha Sachidananda Saraswathi MahaSwamiji is a savvy researcher, superb Jnyaani, and an extremely friendly Guru to every last one. The generous improvement Sreemath has achieved today at a brief period is without a doubt because of MahaSwamiji's heavenly premonition and direction. Sreemath has seen tremendous development in the two its framework and Dharma Prachara exercises under His splendid bearings and productive organization. Holding to Dharma Prachara as the central goal, MahaSwamiji has started numerous inventive tasks of social and profound exercises that serve towards building solidarity and congruity in the general public. Each task hence stretched out by Sreemath has been contributing gigantically to Loka Kshema just as individual edification. Each aficionado who has met MahaSwamiji reports heart-contacting episodes of how MahaSwamiji changed their life and had been a steady heavenly help to them at each point on the schedule. It is surely an exceptionally valuable gift to meet a genuinely holy person of loftiest greatness and significance in the course of one's life.

Early days

Brought into the world in Ulluve, a little villa near Sringeri, His Holiness was named as Nagaraja Sharma in Poorvashrama. Directly from adolescence, He showed no tendency towards material living and was constantly occupied with the consideration of Adhyatmic matters. His unfazed adherence to Dharmic standards and profound commitment to God stuck every individual who met Him. His inborn information and clear comprehension of Veda Sastras even as a kid shocked loved ones. He was additionally a splendid understudy, consistently a clincher at school and school. Be that as it may, every one of these scholastic positions and appreciations scarcely implied anything to Him, who was at that point submerged in the incomparable reality.

The youthful Nagaraja Sharma was profoundly invested in himself and regularly pulled out into isolation. He was commonly discovered lost in contemplation or altogether immersed in Pooja, totally negligent of family or environmental factors. Of the innumerable heavenly episodes that the family had seen during the years gone through with Nagaraja, the sanctification of the Swayambhu Ganapathi sanctum at Ulluve turns into a significant story. Once, when Nagaraja was 13 years of age, He had a fantasy of Lord Ganesha highlighting a spot close by and saying "I'm here. Get me and do Pooja!" The following day Nagaraja tracked down a self-showed divinity (Swayambhu) of Valampuri Ganapathi at exactly the same spot. According to divine bearings, He made a little place of worship close to His home, blessed the god, and began day by day Pooja. This sanctuary of Swayambhu Valampuri Vinayaka is being adored by local people of Ulluve right up 'til the present time.

Commencement into a plain request - Peetarohanam

As years passed, Nagaraja Sharma's inward needing for the Supreme escalated. He stayed free by common names and invested the majority of His energy in comfort, pondering on the Supreme Atma Tattva. He wished to lead an existence of renunciation, in complete detachment from the outside world.

In the long run, He composed a letter to the Sringeri Jagadguru Sri Bharathi Theertha MahaSwamiji, communicating His purpose to consider progressed subjects of Sanskrit, Veda, and Vedanta Shastras. The Sringeri Acharya, who divined the academic ability and intelligence in the youthful Brahmachari, quickly called Him to Sringeri and masterminded His development Vedic learning and practice.

Jagadguru Sri Bharati Theertha MahaSwamiji who was continually directing Nagaraja had noticed His devout, merciful, and pious nature, His sincere craving to help other people, His solid dispassion towards material life, and firm devotion to Dharma. The Jagadguru found in the youthful Brahmachari the heavenly power and astuteness that could lead, guide, and elevate the whole society.

Before long, at the request for the Sringeri Jagadguru Bharathi Theertha MahaSwamiji, on the 21stof May 2001, Sri Nagaraja Sharma was started into Sanyasa and blessed as the Peetadhipathi of the famous Shankaracharya Peetam of Sreemath Hariharapura. Sri Bharathi Theertha Mahaswamiji Himself played out the Pattabhisheka service and reported the youthful renunciate Sri.Nagaraja Sharma as 'Sri Swayampraksha Sachidananda Saraswathi', the Peetadhipathi of Sreemath Hariharapura.

Dharma Prachara

Since the Peetarohanam of MahaSwamiji, there has been colossal improvement in Sreemath's exercises of Dharma Prachara. Lecturing solidarity and uniformity, MahaSwamiji goes all over even to discouraged towns and ghettos for engendering Sanatana Dharma among individuals from varying backgrounds. MahaSwamiji sees unity altogether and goes to each aficionado with much consideration and sympathy.

To dispense with the quickly developing obliviousness among individuals towards our Vedic custom, MahaSwamiji has started various profound exercises that incorporate the Shiva Deeksha program, SriNarasimha Sahasranama Koti Parayana, Vishwa Gayatri Upasak Parishat, Sri LakshmiNarasimha Lekhana Japa Yajnya, and so forth These ventures unite incalculable individuals from various networks and classes under one single rooftop to rehearse Sanatana Dharma with appropriate agreement and belongingness. Zeroing in on otherworldly projects, however, MahaSwamiji has likewise initiated numerous social exercises to help poor people and the destitute. Under the heavenly directions of Swamiji, monetary help is reached out from Sreemath consistently to meriting understudies for higher investigations. Free books are circulated to numerous schools and instructive establishments in far-off regions. Free eye camps are coordinated at towns, where eye test is led for all and scenes are circulated liberated from cost. The clinical uses of numerous helpless families are additionally financed by Sreemath.

Organization

Inside a limited ability to focus, the progress that Sreemath has seen today is enormous. Sreemath's exercises have spread wide and branches have been set up at numerous focuses in South India. The foundation at Hariharapura has likewise improved numerous folds under MahaSwamiji's heavenly headings. For example, when Mahaswamiji rose the Peetam, He understood the require-ment for housing offices for explorers and fans and promptly assembled the 'Lakshmi Nivas' visitor house at Hariharapura. He likewise saw to that day by day Annadanam was accessible for each lover visiting Sreemath, independent of rank or belief. The Brindavana Goshala at Hariharapura, which currently brags of 100+ cows, and the great Someshwara Yagashala at Hariharapura, where Homas and Yajnas are consistently performed consistently, were all Mahaswamiji's initial activities as a Peetadhipathi. MahaSwamiji reproduced the Adhishtana Mandirams of the Parameshti Guru and Paramaguru at Punganoor and Hariharapura separately and furthermore revamped the Swayamprakasha Arsha Vidya Peetam (Vedapatashala) at the banks of Tunga. As of now, under the heavenly direction of MahaSwamiji, the old sanctuary of Sri Sharada LakshmiNarasimha Swamy at Hariharapura is being recreated totally as a stone construction with conventional figures and carvings of perplexing imaginativeness and structural greatness. It is astonishing to watch the sanctuary molding out step by step into a radiant sky rejecting the heavenly home of Lord Sri LakshmiNarasimha and Goddess Sharadambika. MahaKumbhabhishekam of this wonderful sanctuary is intended to be held soon. Additionally, new structures of the Annadana lobby and visitor houses are in development to oblige the expanding number of travelers coming to

Hariharapura. These, however numerous different activities and projects have been refined by Mahaswamiji in a limited capacity to focus. This fantastic advancement that Sreemath has seen today has been conceivable just through MahaSwamiji's heavenly foreknowledge and capable organization.

An intelligent researcher

MahaSwamiji is a researcher second to none, with an excellent capability in different dialects and an immense range of subjects. His basic and clear style of Asirvachanams, clarifying confounded Vedic ideas in straightforward words, draw laymen and researchers the same from all over. The 'SACHIDANANDA VACHANAMRUTAM' a lovely book in Kannada created by MahaSwamiji, scatters Dharmic and Vedic lessons in basic terms that are effectively reasonable to average people. This is a remarkable work that bestows the center goals of Sanatana Dharma and stands truly relatable to each individual independent of sex, local area, religion, position, or doctrine.

Aside from this, there are numerous Krithis and Shlokas made by MahaSwamiji in Sanskrit and Kannada. The creations of MahaSwamiji impart commitment and resonantly express Dharmic standards. They bear an articulate articulation of profoundly complex Vedic ideas with much intellect and grant, additionally kept clear and clear to the comprehension of any lover, be it a researcher or a layman. The Krithi 'Brahmandavanu Bharadi' in recognition of Lord LakshmiNarasimha is a renowned arrangement among aficionados.

My dearest Guru who helped me on the path of becoming whole

MahaSwamiji is an incredible Tapasvi and a humane Guru. Despite the fact that being saturated with thorough Tapas and Anushtanams, MahaSwamiji keeps Himself effectively accessible and congenial to everyone. The cultural contrasts of position, belief, or height are totally unimportant to Him. An exemplification of graciousness and effortlessness, MahaSwamiji goes to each and every aficionado with much love and affection, that aficionados revere Him as the Jaganmatha (Supreme Mother) Herself. A short communication with MahaSwamiji has to be sure to change and raised the existences of many. The rich, poor, instructed, or ignorant, all vibe similarly unique before Swamiji, and offer a cozy holding with Him. His radiating grin and lenient look recuperate the most profound distress and promptly carries satisfaction and harmony to each heart. All the torment and pressing factor brought about by the painful common life turn aimless on arriving at the homestead of MahaSwamiji. At His heavenly presence, one feels the everlasting warmth of adoration and care, such as being settled and lovingly stroked in the defensive arms of the Supreme Mother Herself. The remorseless grasps of material life appear to vanish in a flash. Life effortlessly turns simple and secure when submitted to MahaSwamiji's heavenly direction and assurance. A simple look at this Jagadguru has to be sure been a significant defining moment in the existences of many.

Reworded from as found on https://hariharapura.in/sachidananda_saraswathi

Hail the jagadguru! Sri *Gurave* namaha!